LEARN THE VALUE OF

Determination

◆

by Elaine P. Goley

Illustrated by Deborah Curzon Crocker

◆

ROURKE ENTERPRISES, INC.
VERO BEACH, FL 32964

© 1989 Rourke Enterprises, Inc.

All rights reserved. No part of this book may be reproduced or utilized in any form or by any means, electronic or mechanical including photocopying, recording or by any information storage and retrieval system without permission in writing from the publisher.

Library of Congress Cataloging-in-Publication Data

Goley, Elaine P., 1949–
   Learn the value of determination.

   Summary: Suggests ways we can show determination and accomplishments made possible because others showed determination, such as the invention of the phonograph and landing on the moon.
   1. Perseverance (Ethis)—Juvenile literature.
2. Will—Juvenile literature. [1. Perseverance (Ethics) 2. Conduct of life.] I. Title.
II. Title: Determination.   BJ1533.P4G65
BJ1533.P4G65   1988   179'.9—dc19   88-35316
ISBN 0-86592-389-2

Determination

Do you know what **determination** is?

Learning to read and write takes **determination.**

Determination is practicing your flute every day so that you can play your best in the school concert.

Determination helps your team become better baseball players, so they can get more home runs.

It takes **determination** if you want to win an Olympic gold medal.

. . . and to become one of the world's greatest athletes.

Determination is getting up to try again when you fall off your bike.

When you practice your math lessons every day so that you can get a better grade, that's **determination.**

It takes **determination** to invent something . . .
like the electric light bulb . . .

. . . or to put models together.

Learning to walk takes all of your baby sister's **determination.**

It takes **determination** to learn how to tie your shoes.

It takes **determination** for your brother to get up early every day so that he can deliver papers.

To be a great singing star, you have to have the **determination** to practice long hours.

It takes **determination** to put your clothes away and keep your room clean.

Someone in a wheelchair has to have **determination** to move around on his own like you do.

Eating healthful foods like fruit and nuts instead of candy between meals takes **determination.**

It takes **determination** to write your first book report.

It took **determination** for the pioneers to settle the West.

Determination and hard work got the astronauts to the moon.

Determination is what makes you try harder to learn how to swim.

Determination helps us to do the best that we can and be the best person we can be.

How else can we show **determination?**

Determination

"Mom, mom," cried Sal, "someone stole my skateboard!"

"I can't afford to buy another one," said Mrs. Greco. "Go without one."

I can't go without a skateboard. I'm the neighborhood champ, thought Sal. *I'll buy a new skateboard myself. But where will I get so much money?*

The next day, Sal sold lemonade in front of his house. He made $10. After that, he mowed the neighbor's lawn. He earned another $10. On Saturday, Sal sold nightcrawlers to some fishermen at a nearby lake. Another $10!

"I need $5 more," said Sal to his mom. "What else can I do to earn money?"

"You have a lot of determination," said Mrs. Greco. "I think I can spare $5. Come on. Let's go buy a skateboard."

How did Sal show he had **determination?** What are some ways you have shown **determination?**

Determination

"Let's have a writing contest," said Mrs. Ruiz to her class.

"I've got a great idea for a story," said Debi. "Let's enter the contest, Sue. We might win a prize."

"I'm a bad writer," said Sue.

That night, Debi wrote her story. She looked up hard words in the dictionary. She used lots of action words. Debi wrote some parts of her story over and over.

"I finished my story," Debi said to her dad. "I hope Mrs. Ruiz likes it."

"Did you write your story?" Debi asked Sue on the way to school.

"No, I'd never win," Sue said.

That afternoon, Mrs. Ruiz read the winning story. It was Debi's. Debi felt good. She won some new crayons.

Hard work pays off, Debi thought.

Which girl showed **determination**?
How can being **determined** help you to do better in school?